WISDOM IN CONTRAST

A Life Well Lived?

Victor Grieco

Unless otherwise noted, all Scripture quotations are from the ESV® Bible (The Holy Bible, English Standard Version®), copyright © 2001 by Crossway Bibles, a publishing ministry of Good News Publishers. Used by permission. All rights reserved.

Scripture quotations marked (NIV) are taken from the Holy Bible, New International Version®, NIV®. Copyright © 1973, 1978, 1984, 2011 by Biblica, Inc.™ Used by permission of Zondervan. All rights reserved worldwide. www.zondervan.com. The "NIV" and "New International Version" are trademarks registered in the United States Patent and Trademark Office by Biblica, Inc.™

Scripture quotations marked (AMP) are taken from the Amplified Bible, Copyright © 2015 by The Lockman Foundation. Used by permission.

Copyright © 2023 by Victor Grieco

All rights reserved.

No portion of this book may be reproduced in any form without written permission from the publisher or author, except as permitted by Canadian copyright law.

Book Cover by Al Mahmud (Fiverr graphic designer)
Illustrations by Doan Trang (Fiverr illustrator)

1st edition 2023

CONTENTS

Introduction	5
Tic Toc	6
Two Streams of Thought	9
Bubbles Blowing in the Wind	10
Two Men Died	13
The Circle of Life	16
Playing With Precarious	17
A Smile you Say?	21
Kingship Manifest	22
The Slow Long Road	25
Get Up And Try Again!	30
Up And At It!	32
A Dalliance with Dithering	33
Flowing into Destiny	37
And What Should I Do?	38
She Didn't Care!	43
Of Eagles and Sparrows	48
No Context? Know Context!	49
A Wild Man They Said	53
Active Able Balanced Good	58
Despicable Me?	62
Sometimes Yes! Sometimes No!	62
Find Wisdom Find Life!	68
No Grumpy Snowmen!	73
The Hawk	77
Of No Renown	82
Small Fiefdom Circles Small	86
It Comes With The Job	91
A Spineless Ineffectual Self	94
Fishing	98
Hiding in Plain Sight	100
A Thousand Distant Shores	105
My Champion My Warrior My Strong	109
When the Way Was	115
Dark and Lonely	115
Your Will Be Done!	117
May We Find Him	123
Conclusions	124

Acknowledgements

Thank you Jonathan Willoughby for your excellent editing and formatting guidance!

Thank you to mentors, teachers, parishioners, clients, friends, and all who have encouraged me by expressing your appreciation for words written from my heart to yours!

Dedicated to three wonderful children: Timothy, Lauren and Bethany, you are the light of my life. Thank you for returning love, kindness and grace back into my life, 10 fold!

Introduction

Two great men! Renowned for their wisdom!

One a builder of great cities, fortifications, military capacity, organizing his empire into the richest, and greatest force worldwide. The other an intellectual, a teacher, a leader bringing together rich and poor, slave and free, while sourcing incredible perseverance against all odds.

Two great men! Their recorded thoughts are accurately preserved as guideposts for all who take the time to listen.

Two great men! Both with contrasting views of life.

Gold, silver, precious stones, and the treasures of kings did not suffice to bring peace and contentment to one; instead, filled with despair, he bemoaned life, the afterlife and the futility of life devoid of purpose. The other, a prisoner of the Roman Empire, wrote of great soul-peace! This wise person found every day fulfilling! He was so settled in his personal accomplishments he lost all fear of death, making claims that an afterlife was his to anticipate.

In the pages that follow I hope to affect the despairing emotion of the one, the triumph of the other, and the good wisdom of both.

The question remains: What of my life? Will it be a *"Life well Lived?"*

Tic Toc

What has been is what will be, and what has been done is what will be done, and there is nothing new under the sun.
Ecclesiastes 1:9

The watchmaker looked:
Tic Toc Tic Toc
The second hand swept again,
Tic Toc Tic Toc

And when two hands met
At highest point
A boom alerted,
All who in attentive
Posture cocked
Their heads and wondered
At the time:
Tic Toc Tic Toc

Again, the second hand went by:
Tic Toc Tic Toc

Yet again the wheel
Within the wheel
Ground out a minute more:
Tic Toc Tic Toc
In days gone by
the watchmaker's
Undiscovered knowledge
Of that time piece,
Meant acceptance
Of the hour:
Tic Toc Tic Toc

Yet even now
The watchmaker,
Knew the wisdom
Garnered in his
More educated state,
Of how the inner workings
Operated within that
Crystal gold circumference,
Would not stop the
Endless passing of the time
Tic Toc Tic Toc
Education of itself,
Brings no relief

From the unrelenting
Pass of time:
Tic Toc Tic Toc

His focused knowledge,
Stilled no angry surge
As reality itself
Smirked and mocked
That nothing could be done
To stop the never ending
Passing of the time:
Tic Toc Tic Toc

Relentless sweeping
Of the hour's arm
While Minutes added up
From seconds
Yet it goes again:
Tic Toc Tic Toc

Oh will it ever stop?

Tic Toc Tic Toc
Tic Toc Tic Toc

Oh will it ever stop?

Tic Toc Tic Toc
Tic Toc Tic Toc

———

Two Streams of Thought

I read about this vast universe and see it with my own eyes in the night sky. I, an infinitesimal speck on this revolving planet burdened with the task of making sense of it all. At times a heavy, heavy, burden as the planet on which I dwell turns endless circles day after day year after year. Like a molecule of water rushing to the ocean, evaporating, carried on the winds, crystalizing and falling as snow into a river only to rush to the ocean again and again and again in meaningless endless cycles.

. . . But then another way of thinking. An attitude instilled by values ceded deep within my soul by God and Christian family: I am here to achieve to accomplish to love and be loved. I am tasked with a delightful life. One that allows me to watch as lives around me are blessed at work, in friendship and in family. I am here to protect others, holding the hand of someone who suffers, crying with those who cry, while smiling in the face of death itself. I am not here by some chance encounter; but by destiny planned before the universe was born.

Two streams of thought. One of chance, the other of great purpose; yet only one choice to be made!

Bubbles Blowing in the Wind

So I became great and surpassed all who were before me in Jerusalem. Also my wisdom remained with me. And whatever my eyes desired I did not keep from them... and behold, all was vanity and a striving after wind, and there was nothing to be gained under the sun.
Ecclesiastes 2:9-11

The field was beautiful
Dressed in finest
Flowers bright
Red yellow orange
And purple fare

The child young and
Playful skipped
The grassy valley
Smiling as she reached for
Perfect globes
Floating shoulder height
Produced by
Circles dipped in
Soapy mixture
Held aloft
Suspended
Colours of the rainbow
Breezed a step ahead
Running jumping
Sure to catch
the biggest of them all
She followed
Course of gentle wind

And then she
stopped!
The smile left

It was the smallest
Most insignificant
And tender touch
That made the
Bubble disappear.

That's when
Wisdom spoke its
Stark reality
To desires hidden deep
Within my heart;
"The bubble bursts,
When it is all
I ever chase!"

The bubble bursts
When like a child,
I grasp it
Convinced it brings relief.

There must be
More than soapy
Insignificance
Evaporating with
No consideration
For the chasing

There must be
More than
Bubbles
Bubbles bursting
In the wind!

Two Men Died

The wise have eyes in their heads, while the fool walks in the darkness; but I came to realize that the same fate overtakes them both. Ecclesiastes 2:14 NIV

Two men died

One birthed
strong and mighty
Roamed the plains
Tracking stealthy
Game

Another in his
Office tower
Educated bright
And dressed for dinner
Understood the
Secrets of great books

Two men died

Both were praised
And both
Commended for
Their actions
Great and small

Two men died

And while
One knew how

To sky scrape cities
The other's only
Claim to fame
Was knowing how
To downwind from
Gazelle

Two men died

And some ignored
The fact
While others mourned
And cried

Yet two men died.

Two men died
And there was

No one who
Would ever
Sky scrape like the one

Two men died
And there was
No one who
Would ever
Downwind like the other.

Yes two men died
And when they did
They left it
ALL behind

The Circle of Life

Empires come and Empires go!

The circle of life screams: "Even mighty pyramids crumble."

Some shrug the thought away. Others cry.

Many despair; "You mean after a lifetime of work, the storms of life, the rise and fall of nations, the sleet of time erodes all accomplishment?"

"Yes! It will!" laughs destiny.

Then a quiet voice: "There are many actions that build a different structure! Eternally safe. Invisible to the naked eye."

And that quiet voice whispers: "The best investments are those quietly made in the lives of other people in honour of the One who came to redeem them great and small."

Playing With Precarious

He has made everything beautiful in its time. Also, he has put eternity into man's heart, yet so that he cannot find out what God has done from the beginning to the end.
Ecclesiastes 3:11

Does the right now
Of right now
Help me know
The not yet
Of eternity?

Can a person
Bound by time
Know a taste
Yes! Just a taste,
Of Eternity so vast and wide?
Eternity that never can be fathomed?

Perhaps, just maybe
Time does taste
Eternity when
One looks back
On deeds
Invested in the lives
Of those
Less fortunate?

Or maybe on
A wire high above
An overhanging cliff that
Dares defy the downward

Drag of gravity while
Playing with precarious?

Does a taste of Time
Give way to
A glimpse
(However small)
Of Eternity
So long?

Does time
Itself allow for me a

Backward ever
Or a forward
Till there is
No more?

Does the right now
Of right now
Help me know
The not yet
Of eternity?

Perhaps the taste
Yes just a taste
Will come from knowledge
That the One who fashioned
Deep within the womb
Used building blocks
Of personality
To knit Goodness
Together with
Determinations
Yet to be unfolded
Eventually to be displayed
On the road right
Now, even perhaps
While playing with
Precarious, Yet
Destined be expressed,
For all to see
In eternity
So long,

It can ne'er be grasped right now
No never grasped right now!

Yet Eternity …
Is!
And evermore
Shall be!

A Smile you Say?

Magnificent opportunities they bring. I've done nothing to deserve them. Two friends or foes depending on their use. Such are both the gift of time and of choice.

They intersect and cause joy or sorrow. The proper use of a smile will bless a life. The wrong use may be interpreted as a smirk and cause great pain. The smile as does a frown, needs the proper time and context to be expressed.

Some days I wonder if I will ever get it right. I move through life's most precious commodity: time. And while I do there are choices to be made: a time and a place for every smile, every handshake, every word of advice. Like sand moving from one section of the hourglass to the other, each choice made in time will bring change. May my choices be right. May they be wise. Today. Everyday.

———

Kingship Manifest

But God, being rich in mercy, because of the great love with which he loved us, even when we were dead in our trespasses, made us alive together with Christ – by grace you have been saved – and raised us up with him and seated us with him in the heavenly places in Christ Jesus.
Ephesians 2:4-6

Some observe a weak
Pathetic beggar
Concluding that He
Stumbled to a pointless
Weak and sickly
Death

Yet I?
Yes, I do cherish,
Kingship manifest
In destiny
So right

He high stepped
Over galaxies
Ignoring black hole
Radiated dangers,
As though but puddles small!

The universe itself
Yielded to its owner,
Gaining entrance through
The humble doorway
Of a virgin's womb.
In all His majesty
He smiled even while the

Threats of angry mobs
Rang out towards
The patient presentation
Of His spoken truth

Majestically with
Purpose he allowed
The Jewish throngs and
Roman soldiers curse
Him and abuse
His loving sacrificial act.

Yet I?
Yes, I do cherish,
Kingship Manifest
For me

Some cursed
His forgiveness
Thrust
Towards them
On His cross

Others took a
Spear and while
They mocked,
His plight they
Pierced his side!

Yet I?
Yes, I do cherish,
Kingship Manifest
For me.

Many mock Him,
Snubbing His

Arrival and
Ignoring all
He did!

Others do not
Care he healed
The sick or
Raised the
Dead.

Yet I?
Yes, I do cherish,
Kingship manifest
for me.

Of all the
Lost and lonely souls
Venting anger
At Him
I was one,
Yes, I was one!

And yet he took me
By the hand
And let me walk
With Him
As if a prince!
Yes, I walk as if
A prince.

So, I
Yes, I do cherish,
Kingship manifest
For me

The Slow Long Road

*Again I saw all the oppressions that are done under the sun.
And behold, the tears of the oppressed, and they had no one
to comfort them! Ecclesiastes 4:1*

Stumbling down the
Long and dusty
Road
The traveler
Realized the way
Was filled with
Unanticipated dangers
Which destroyed
Most of those
Who traveled there before.

But that very traveler
Could, if he
But would,
Ask direction from above
To find a way,
And make it safely
To the other side.

The traveler found
The way was much longer
Then supplies
Could ever last

But those that
Travelled could,
If they but would,

Find a way
With no supplies.

But most would not!
No!
Most would not!

A wise man spoke
To those along that road and said
There were those who had
A way to get safely
To the destination
Despite the
Dangers of the road.

That wise man said there
Are those few
Who find safe passage
To the other side
Those few that do,
Incorporate a
Secret wisdom
Full of understanding
How to complete
The dreadful trip.

But most would not
Go the way
That wise man
Did prescribe.
These all ignored
The wisdom
And cursed
The aggravation of the road.

Only a few others
Found the Wisdom
Spoken from above!
These realize the potential,
Of that flowing
Secret strength

Sadly most do not
Find the secret wisdom
Promised to them
From above
And these many
Are the lost
And weary travelers
That could stop
Their stumbling on their way
If they would
But they don't
Because they won't

Yet others few in number,
Find much
Wisdom from above.
These look
Because they can
And when they do
They find
Simple answers
Which help them
Make it safely
To the other side

These few speak of
Care and comfort
That turns dangers
Into conquests
Their truth
They say,
Can easily be found
And they do
Make it to the
Other side

The millions never
Listening to the
Wisdom from above
Are lost and
Stumbling on their way
They too can
Find it
If they would
But they don't
Because they won't!

Yet even these many
Who don't
Because they won't
Are yet still invited
To mine the secret
Wisdom at the source.

Yet a small few others
Look up
And ask direction
From the Source where
Wisdom helps them
Find the answers,
Most others do not find.

And then these few
Who find the secret
Walk on wisdom's pathways
These few
Who find the secret
Make it safely
To the other side.

Wisdom has built her house; she has hewn her seven pillars.
She has slaughtered her beasts; she has mixed her wine; she has also set her table.
She has sent out her young women to call from the highest places in the town, "Whoever is simple, let him turn in here!"
Proverbs 9:1-4

Get Up And Try Again!

Two are better than one, because they have a good return for their labor: If either of them falls down, one can help the other up. But pity anyone who falls and has no one to help them up. Ecclesiastes 4:9-10

Young man young woman
Get up and try again!

All who walked
This path
Before you
Had a stumble and a fall!

No one liked it
When pain came
And many
Fainted on the way.

But young man
Young woman
You have a resource
You can access
When the way ahead is tough

So when success eludes you
And you rise to try again
There's a partner
Waiting willing lifting
Those who rise
From failure dark.
Young man young woman
Get up and try again!

Young man young woman
There is One
Who is an expert
Helping those
Who rise and
Look for help!

Defeat is not
Your destiny
Nor discouragement
Your lot!

Get to know the One
Who's promise
Let's you
Rise from ashes grim.

Young man young woman
There's one
That offers you His hand!

Have you ever
Asked His guidance
When confused by
Murky fog?

He is there
And ready for you,
Now giving you
His hand

Young man, young woman!
Get up and try again!

Up And At It!

How ironic! It is not always the most talent that lands the job, not always the smartest that makes the best decision, not always the strongest that wins the fight nor the fastest that wins the race.

Today like every day I will face challenges. It is humbling to know I am not the 'best' equipped to do the tasks before me. Others are faster, brighter, younger and more talented but the challenges I face are mine and mine alone. What am I to do? The perfectionist in me thinks I should not even bother; after all, others can do it better. But that is not what I do; I get up, go to work, put on my 'big boy clothes' and do my best. I do that over and over again. That is called "Faith". I believe that I can accomplish something good even though others may be able to do better.

Once in a while the scoreboard of life shows me the results. Guess what? Much to my surprise, on rare occasions I discover I am in first place!

What if I shriveled at the challenge? What if adopted the attitude that because there are others that are smarter and brighter and more charismatic, I would not try? What if I did not let the seeds of hope grow into persistent faith?

Faith brings into reality the opportunity to succeed: Do it!

———

Again I saw that under the sun the race is not to the swift, nor the battle to the strong, nor bread to the wise, nor riches to the intelligent, nor favor to those with knowledge, but time and chance happen to them all. Ecclesiastes 9:11

A Dalliance with Dithering

A dalliance
With dithering,
While doubting every
Second guessed decision
Was the game
Confusion played!

Until one day
A revelation that
Devine direction
Always hides
behind the simple
Things of life

A confidence and trust
Began to grow
Replacing troubled thoughts
With new and clear direction

Some days a thought
Birthed in the daily
Reading

Other times a word
Encased in glass
And glowing
Like a ruby
Red and warm,
Now spoken by a friend
Or some other caring
Person met along the way.

Delightful
Guidance of
A friend or two,
Brings a deep and
Settled calm.

And the calm
Was also there,
Because a purposed
Understanding of the
Tremendous confidence
That guidance given
From above cannot be
Purchased by some
Great achievement or
Other philanthropic act.

No!
Guidance is
A gift
Received with wonder
Like a child
Unwrapping presents
On their day!

This now
My paradigm of
Understanding that
A yielded life to
Higher power
Brings with it
Wisdom of
The next best thing
To do

No longer
Should we wonder
Anymore at
What? and why? and How?

Now we know
It's possible for
Good decisions
To be made!

They can:
When with an inner
Yielded posture of surrender
We look
To the creative
Strength of
One who
Has all power

And then with
Confidence and faith
Step out:
Because we can!
Step out:
Because we are not alone!
Step out:
And walk with Him!

On waters deep
We do step out!

We step out
With inner
Yielded confidence
To the creative
Strength of
One who
Has all power

Yes we
Go forward
Without fear!

We go forward
Wisdom leading us
As we with confidence,
We do Step out!

Step out!

We will
Step out!

Flowing into Destiny

A stream in the forest does not wonder which direction to go. Gravity and the lay of the land provide the path ahead. Sometimes life is like that. A small choice in our education, a first job, convictions of a good conscience, a chance meeting which turns into enduring romance, the love of family and the good counsel of friends are like the banks of a river providing invisible boundaries that give us direction.

Great people understand that divine direction does not come in the form of a booming voice; instead, it whispers softly, ever so incrementally helping us travel to our destination, always consistent with the principles in Scripture. Great people learn that wisdom often comes from the very people who have proven they really care!

God's means of providing guidance is like the banks of a river, all of which the God of the Universe uses to help us on our way!

Trust in the Lord with all your heart, and do not lean on your own understanding. In all your ways acknowledge him, and he will make straight your paths. Proverbs 3:5-6

And What Should I Do?

If you see in a province the oppression of the poor and the violation of justice and righteousness, do not be amazed at the matter. Ecclesiastes 5:8

And what should I do?
When all around
Are hungry mouths to feed?

And what should I do
When criminals
Suppress and bind
The weak to
Bonds that never
Break?

What should I do
When I know of
A man that beat his
Family down?

And what should I do?
When there are
Those who live
Inciting riot
In the street?

And what should I do
When just a taste
Leads throngs
To lifelong cravings
Never satisfied?
I see it all

And when I do
There is a part
Down deep inside
That shrinks so small
And insignificant
I say, "I think,
I know
I cannot do."

But then I look
Before me and
As far as ocean
Wide I see a
Thousand billion
Opportunities to
Help one here
And there and everywhere
Before me
Like a million
Thousand billion
Pebbles on a beach

Now I know
What I should do!

And so, I do!

Yes, now I know
There is one
Step that I can take,
To make one small
And seeming
Insignificant soul
A better state.

Yes, now I know
What I should do
And so, I do!

I go and do
One little
Thing so
Small that
Only the most
Hopeful ever
Think it might
Yet make a
Difference in the dark!

Yes, I do know
What I should do!
So, I do
What I
Should do!

I see a thousand billion
Acts of kindness
Not yet done,

And what I do
Is to do,
But one!

And that one
Act that I can do,
In the space
Before me
On my way:
I do!

I do because
I can,

I do
Because the one
Small act of kindness
Will be one that
Makes a difference
To the one
To whom it's
Done!

Yes, one received it
On that day,

They received
It and it meant
Relief!

Yes I do know
Now what to do
and so, I do!

And so, I do!

*And whoever gives one of these little ones
even a cup of cold water because he is a disciple,
truly, I say to you, he will by no means lose his reward.
Matthew 10:42*

She Didn't Care!

There is an evil that I have seen under the sun, and it lies heavy on mankind: a man to whom God gives wealth, possessions, and honor, so that he lacks nothing of all that he desires, yet God does not give him power to enjoy them, but a stranger enjoys them. This is vanity; it is a grievous evil.
Ecclesiastes 6:1-2

She walked the
Hollow sounding
Marbled hallway of the
great stone mansion
Where once three
Children played.

Dressed a wardrobe
Oxymoron
With a track suit
And high heels
But these days nothing
Seemed worth
A dress
Or even makeup
Anymore
She didn't care!

She didn't care!

Her high heeled
Steps echoed off
The granite stones
As she deftly plodded
Across the great hall

There was a
Time when she would
Stop to admire
The sparkling beauty of
The crystal golden chandelier
In all its grandeur.

But never since the
Money wars,
Was there desire
To take any
Time to pause.

She saw
No pleasure in it
Anymore,
She didn't care.

She didn't care.

As she swung
Open the heavy
Door leading to the
Pristine clean
Cavernous garage

She sighed,
She didn't care.

The four cars
In the underground
Necessitated decision at
Departure,
Always complicated,
By what impression she

Would make with
The car she chose to drive

She stood at the doorway
Staring at the cars.

Simple decisions
For any reason
Caused her pain.

These dark days
Going to the office
Registered a tedious task.

She stared unmoving,
She didn't care.

She didn't care.

Instead of driving to
Her towered office
She turned away from
The garage and
Sent a text,
Instructing her pilot
To ready the
Helicopter on the roof

It was that
Time of year when
Blackouts lifted,
Allowing her to
Exercise options
On the rising Stock
Worth 450 million now.

She deemed it
Such a chore.
She didn't care.

She didn't care.

Profits, profits, profits,
Boring profits!

And what good
Would all the
Profits do,
When hers seemed
A forever
Morose and
Melancholic state?

And most of all
Like all that lay
Before her now
She didn't care.

She didn't care.

Of Eagles and Sparrows

Once upon a time there was an eagle with the heart of a sparrow. Said eagle fluttered from building to building looking for scraps on the barnyard floor.
One day a dominating screech high in the sky invited the eagle to rise on the wings of the wind but our poor sparrow-eagle was sure it could not fly higher than the peak of the barn. It lived out its days eking out a sparrow's existence.

Once upon a time there was an eagle with the heart of a sparrow. Said eagle fluttered from building to building looking for scraps on the barnyard floor.
One day a dominating screech high in the sky invited the eagle to rise on the wings of the wind; with mighty majesty the eagle left behind the pecking life of sparrow-hood, circling ever upward towards the sun.

There are times in my life when I am sure that the barnyard sets my boundary and sure enough, like a self-fulfilling prophesy, the barnyard does set my limits!

At other times I have acknowledged the eagle's heart within.

Today I have a choice: Say "yes" to the call from above . . . or not! May the eagle's heart be mine!

And to know the love of Christ that surpasses knowledge, that you may be filled with all the fullness of God.
Ephesians 3:19

No Context? Know Context!

*All the toil of man is for his mouth,
yet his appetite is not satisfied.
Ecclesiastes 6:7*

If I were just a taste bud
I couldn't let you know
How this morsel
Compared to that
For a taste bud with
No mind
Has but a function to
Assess
But that function
Stands alone
When it no
Context knows

And my enjoyment
Of what passed
My lips
Would not be mine
For though I
Taste, I would not
Know what enjoyment
Even was.

Or perhaps if I were
A thousand nerve
Endings on the tip
Of a finger
I could measure texture
Rough or smooth
But on my own

Without a mind
I could not
Tell you any
Benefit it brought

Or if I engage in
Sex for pleasure
That is
Mine and mine alone,
Riding the thrill of it
With no commitment
Forever strong or true,
I again would be a
Mindless tastebud
Who trained itself
To know pleasure
Without context
Or feeling without mind.

If I made millions,
Many millions
Amassing fortune
For myself
Then yet again
Without a context
Of my purpose
In its' earning,
What use would
It all be?

I'd only know
I had enough to eat
Another day.

I was designed

For more than
Feeling measured feelings
On a day
Encased in time.

There is a spirit
And a mind that is
Attached to measured
Feelings
One that brings
Reality of every
Feeling into
Context-u-alized
Purpose for my life

And so I strive
For one thing only
And that above all else
I look and wonder
At this quest now
Laid before me
As a great and special challenge

My quest is Knowing

Knowing with a
Deep down understanding,
At the reason for my being!

Communing with
The God of heaven
Earth and sky
To know His
Purpose meant
For me,

And even while
I do not fully
Understand,
That good search
Towards the God
Of heaven will
Of itself bring
Broader meaning
To the tastebud
And the wealth
And all the
Tingling feelings
Of a life that
Has a context
Rooted in
Eternal fact.

Now to him who is able to do far more abundantly than all that we ask or think, according to the power at work within us, to him be glory in the church and in Christ Jesus throughout all generations, forever and ever. Amen.
Ephesians 3:20-21

A WILD MAN THEY SAID

The words of the wise heard in quiet are better than the shouting of a ruler among fools Ecclesiastes 9:17

A wild man
They said;
Demanding, curt, driven!

Qualities needed
In his tough
Construction world

His bosses liked
Him at the first
He produced and drove
The workers
Complete all projects
Large or small
And that they did it all
Before deadlines came and went

And even more. . .
All with excellent
Good quality
On top of every early
Or on time completion:

Nothing like that
Ever done before,
They said!

Outstanding,
They said!

Until the day
He went too far
With wild driving yelling
At the workers on the job
His Hurtful pressure went too far
And workers had enough

They left to
Help the
Competition reach
The top

And that was that;
His contract ended,
So they said!

What should he do?
He could not dig
To beg he was
Ashamed.

And then he
Knew what he would do!
He Left the house
Each day the way he did before,
Helped with planners
On the job
Wherever
Projects plenty
Ran into
A challenge
Large or small!

He brought experience,
And freely gave his time,

And when these
Voluntary jobs
Were greatly helped,
He won admiration from
His peers
Who once wondered how he
Did what he did do

So the wild man
Now had a group of friends,
They said!

And another thing
That happened
To this wild
Yelling boss
Was that he
Learned to care
About the workers
On the job

And all this
That helped the
Wild man to
Start again,
They said!

I knew another man
Who lost a job,
That man could
Not do the things
He did before,
They said!
Disqualified,
They said!

And shamed
Down to the core
He also knew
He could not dig
And to beg
He was ashamed!

But he decided
Ask his God
That whether
Large or small
He would help
Where ere he could.

No one knows the many
Things this man has done,
The people who
Once said that
He should be
Disqualified
Will never know!

But in his own way,
And with God's help
This man has
Done what
Few have done,
No matter what
They said!
No matter what
They said!

*And the manager said to himself,
'What shall I do, since my master
is taking the management away from me?
I am not strong enough to dig,
and I am ashamed to beg.
Luke 16:3*

Active Able Balanced Good

Say not, "Why were the former days better than these?" For it is not from wisdom that you ask this. In the day of prosperity be joyful, and in the day of adversity consider: God has made the one as well as the other.
Ecclesiastes 7:1,14a.

If my mind
Is active,
Able
Balanced
And good.

It then takes all
Of life's small things:
The insignificant
Breath of a wind
Wafting through
Pine needles
Spreading the sweet
Odour of
The great outdoors
And transforms that scent
Into smiles
Of transformational
Delight!

If my mind
Is active,
Able
Balanced
Good.

It then takes all
Of life's small things:
The look of love
As tender eyes
Respond to bended knee,
And diamond holding hand
Extended in an ask.
And hears the
Wonderous whispered
"Yes"!

If my mind
Is active,
Able
Balanced
Good.

It then takes all
Of life's small things:
Like the
Energetic bouncing
Of children
Cousins wildly
Running circles
In a stately home,
And turns the
Chaos into
Warmth of family
Love!

If my mind
Is active,
Able
Balanced
Good.

It then takes all
Of life's small things:
Like the
Sparkling falling
Snow that
Drifts the driveway
Into laborious
Shovel lifting
Work
And laughs at
Mother nature's
White blanket
Winter contribution.

If my mind
Is active,
Able
Balanced
Good.

It then takes all
Of life's small things:

And values high
Unnoticed virtues
Many times
Forgotten midst
The busyness of life.

If my mind
Is active,
Able
Balanced
Good.

Then that
Of and
In itself
Is un-forecasted
Greatness!
Yes!
A dream lived
Out in time!

Despicable Me?
Sometimes Yes! Sometimes No!

*Be not overly righteous, and do not make yourself too wise.
Why should you destroy yourself? Be not overly wicked,
neither be a fool. Why should you die before your time?
Ecclesiastes 7:16-17*

If I came across
Like I was better
Than all others
Living life within
My circle,
Especially if there
Was a possibility
No matter how
Small it might be,
That my actions
Or my words
Portrayed a better
Than another attitude

Then that would be
A sad commentary indeed
For I am in no way
Better than those
Fighting life
While standing
Next to me

I must be sure
To make it clear
That I am no better
Than any person
Living next to me

And please know
That if by chance
I came into your hearing
With a solution
To your burden
It was more
Because I learned
A thing or two
When life had laid
Me low
And bad choices
Maximized my pain
Than that I think
That I am smarter
Or better
Stronger or wiser
Than others
Standing by
Including you

Please understand
It's not because
I am smarter or
Wiser or that I have
Some brilliance
Better

And so I must be sure
Yes very sure
To make it clear
That I am no better
Than the other standing
Next to me.

And If my stumbling
Words gave
Those who heard them
The thought that
I deemed my
Life better than
They were, then
I have miserably failed
To speak my truth
In a clear and
Concise way
And once again
I must admit that
Eloquence itself
Has failed my
Feeble lips

I am no better
Than the person
Next to me
I must be clear
For I am not
No I am not.

But yet again
A sister thought
That even though
I'm not . . .
. . . I am a person
With my own gifts
Which like a tool
Fashioned for a
Purpose
Like a brush
Applying artists' paint

When I'm led
And guided from above
There are things
Specially set out
For me that I am
Able with His help
To do

I am a person
With a purpose
Fashioned for tasks
Requiring guidance
From the One above
Who knows just why
He made my life
With all its gifting
Great and small

And when with
Humble heart
I put my hand
In His,
I find the Master Artist
Fashions pictures`
Beautiful that blend
With other colours
Painted on that canvas
Long before my time.

I find in myself
The weaknesses are
There to teach me
That the one above
Has strengths that
Match those weak things
That in myself I dread.

And what he does is
Take those things
That I despise
And fashions out
A purpose that
With His help
Will let me be
A servant to the ones
Within arm's reach

So if I came across
Like I was better
Than all others
Living life within
My circle,
Especially if there

Was a possibility
No matter how
Small it might be,
That my actions
Or my words
Portrayed a better
Than another attitude
When truth be told
I am in no way
Better than those
Fighting life
While standing
Next to me
Especially
When all that
I've been commissioned
Yet to do
Is to truly be
A servant to the ones
Within arm's reach

A servant to the ones
Within arm's reach
Knowing indeed
I am no better
Than the others
Standing next to me

---

*But grace was given to each one of us
according to the measure of Christ's gift.
Ephesians 4:7*

Find Wisdom Find Life!

Who is like the wise?
And who knows the interpretation of a thing?
A man's wisdom makes his face shine,
and the hardness of his face is changed.
Ecclesiastes 8:1

In that dark
Mysterious moment
Between the darkness
And the light

Unravelling wisdom
Spoke its secrets
Strong
In silence to my soul

There I learned
Of things profoundly
Fashioned deep
Down, down.
Down so deep
In cavernous
Depths of
Mysterious understanding.

Things I never
Thought or mused
Because the busy
Tempo robbed
My hearing
And my Understanding,

'Til I despaired to
Know what I should know

But in that dark
Mysterious moment
Between the darkness
And the light

The Solitude
and solace
Spoke clear truth
To what had
long time been
A darkly cluttered mind

So in this
Loudly quiet moment
Between deep
Sleep darkness
And the light

The stillness whispers
Softly telling secrets
Mined eternal
In the Depth of
Jeweled Insight
Tumbling over formulated
Theorems of the solid
Rock of my set ways
Traditions never bent
Resisting strong

Yet now this wisdom
Like a brightness

Dawns my soul
With insights
never seen before

And so the still
Small and quiet voice
Of that secret place
Between
the darkness and the light

Teaches my
Stubborn heart
What books and
Lectures never could

All in that dark
Mysterious moment
Between the darkness
And the light

When the spoke
Word of eternal truth
I embrace as
Treasured wisdom strong,
My eyes they
Brighten granting
Good direction
To my aching soul.

Now the glorious path ahead
Stands in great
Contrast to what was
My darkly troubled soul

All in that
Darkly quiet moment
Between the darkness
And the light

When shouting
Whispers speak
Direction giving
Treasured wisdom
Strong

All in that
Darkly quiet moment
Between the darkness
And the light

———————

*For God speaks in one way,
and in two, though man does not perceive it.
In a dream, in a vision of the night,
when deep sleep falls on men,
while they slumber on their beds,
Job 33:14-16*

No Grumpy Snowmen!

So I commend the enjoyment of life, because there is nothing better for a person under the sun than to eat and drink and be glad. Then joy will accompany them in their toil all the days of the life God has given them under the sun.
Ecclesiastes 8:15 NIV

Folded arms!
Grumpy!
After all, Life isn't fair
Don't you know?

Sometimes the bad
Get what
The good deserve!

Sometimes the good
Get what
The bad deserve

So no wonder
I'm folded arms and
Grumpy! Angry! Grumpy!

After all. ..
. . . Life isn't fair!
Don't you know?

So no wonder
I'm folded arms and
Grumpy! Angry! Grumpy!

Yet through it all
The sun shines bright
For children who do
Dance in warm ocean waves

And half a world away
Other kids play
And pack white bright snow
Into small forts,
And make snowmen
On the lawn
And lying on the
Snow packed ground
They laugh with glee
At Angel impressions
In the dimpled
sparkling crystals white.

The children know
What folded adults don't
Life isn't fair:
"So What?" To that!

The children know
That in the midst of
Chaos in stern
Judgement chambers
There are still
Waves that beat on
Sandy shores

The children know
That even when
Bad is done to good
And good to bad,

There always is
A carrot one can
Put on a snowman's
Smiling face.

And who are we to think
With folded arms
And furrowed brows
That kids are wrong
And we are right?

Who are we to think
They should be us
And not us them?

Maybe the time
Has come to let
Our ego down, unfold our arms
And let life's lesson
Teach us what the
Children know!

Yes sometimes wrong
Is done to good
And bad is done
To right

But still the
Sun does glisten
Off the crest of every wave
And still the snow
Does sparkle like
A thousand million
Diamonds brighter
Than the stars at
Darkest night

And who are we to think
With folded arms
And furrowed brows
That kids are wrong
And we are right?

Rejoice in the Lord always; again I will say, rejoice.
Philippians 4:4

The Hawk

*. . . the race is not to the swift, nor the battle to the strong,
nor bread to the wise, nor riches to the intelligent, nor favor
to those with knowledge, but time and chance happen to
them all. For man does not know his time . . .*
Ecclesiastes 9:11-12

The hawk it
soared up higher.
On the wings of wind
It circled!

While down below
Red breast hopping bird,
Went about its
Early morning hunt
Midst dew drenched grass,
Not knowing danger
High above
Observed its'
Every move.

As quickly as a
Fly's wing
Beats a stroke,
Life was wrest
From that pretty
Little bird
That used to
Hop along the
Dew drenched grass!

And maybe just for me God
Made the hawk to fly

Maybe just so
I could be reminded,
How I never know,
If this or that
Or maybe another
Instant moment
In one split second
(Never thought it
Ever could be so),
But maybe just so
I could be reminded,
How in one
Brief breath of time
My life could end,
And I might be
Like all history
Gone before.

I - a memory for those
Who choose to
Think of who I am,
Or what I ever was.

A memory for some
I dared to breach,
With arrogance or
Hurt or other
Dark and dismal
Thought

Yet others still
A memory
Of love
And noble
Cause

But just the same
Maybe that
Hawk that soars
Up in the sky,
Is for me
So, I can understand,
How frail life is;
How unexpected it
Will always be for
Those who care to
Take a moment
Of their time
To understand
To really, fully, understand.

This moment
We NOW
Have,
This moment,
(Never guaranteed
Another)!

Maybe that Hawk
Is there so I
Can know that I
Myself do
Live this moment
Free,
But never
Guaranteed another.

Maybe that hawk
Does let me
Know that any
Speaking voice
I have with God
above will be
For me
The most important
Instant of
this very
Moment
While today is
Called today!

Maybe that Hawk
Is there so I
Can know
These things and prosper

Strong in all
The moments
Left for me
For all I
Can yet be and do
According to
The purpose set
For me
By the one
Who gifted me
With vision clear
Granted by
The One who
Made the
Hawk and
Pretty red breast bird
So I can know
So I can know!

Therefore be imitators of God,
as beloved children.
And walk in love,
as Christ loved us
and gave himself up for us,
a fragrant offering and sacrifice to God.
Ephesians 5:1-2

Of No Renown

*There was a little city with few men in it,
and a great king came against it and besieged it,
building great siegeworks against it.
But there was found in it a poor, wise man,
and he by his wisdom delivered the city.
Yet no one remembered that poor man.
Ecclesiastes 9:14-15*

The problem was great
The person was small
A huge crisis
They said
With no solution
At all

Movers and shakers
Thought they could
Turn that situation
Into gold
But soon found out
Their best brought
to the table only made
The troubling matters worse

The problem was great
The person was small
A huge crisis
They said
With no solution
At all

Unexpected wisdom
Came from
A small small corner
Devoid of notoriety
Or any recognition
Yet the profound
Answer given
Simply explained
The solution everyone sought

The problem was great
The person was small
A huge crisis
They said
With no solution
At all

The best way to go
Outlined with
Deft small directives
Which when followed
Brought solution
To the quandary

The problem was great
The person was small
A huge crisis
They said
With no solution
At all

Movers and shakers
Stepped aside
When everyone tried

To honour the one
Who had the wisdom
And the smarts to
Bring resolution to
The situation

But the person with the answer
Could not be found
Else but back in their
Small small corner
Devoid of notoriety

And that's the way
He liked it!
Alone by his own sweet self
With peace
And safety all around

No fanfare
No glorious moment
Just a simple
Small small corner
At the back
And that's why he smiled
On and on . ..

Because he
Wanted it to be
That way. . .

The problem was great
The person was small
A huge crisis
They said
With no solution
At all

Until the one
In the corner
At the back
Made it
No problem at all!

Postscript: ***Be the one in the corner***

Small Fiefdom Circles Small

Dead flies make the perfumer's ointment give off a stench;
so a little folly outweighs wisdom and honor.
Even when the fool walks on the road, he lacks sense, and he
says to everyone that he is a fool.
Ecclesiastes 10:1,3

Those in that peer group
Small called it
A kingdom
Small
But I thought
Maybe
A fiefdom was more
Like it

A small small
Circle small of influence
With like small minded
People idolizing
The idiot at the top
Is what it was.

Everyone patting
Each other on the back
Did make them
Think that they were
All right
Alright

Can you believe,
in their small
Non influential circle
Each thought the other

A bright and shining star,
While holding out
In special wonder
The dumb idiot
At the top?

I mock their circle small
I do!
I mock it with a haughty
Snort!
And just about to
Turn and walk away
I look again
And there I am!

I found my own circle
Slapping others on
The back
While taking queues
From whatever idiot
Is at the top today!

Then stepping back
I see small circles
Everywhere with people
Looking down
With distain on
All others in any
Circle not
Their own

And suddenly I
Realize the ironic
Predic-a-ment
Of it all

Each in our own small
And haughty circle
pats each other
On the back,
While affirming
Staunch and stalwart
Theory of how to
Do life better than
The other.
Each thinks ourselves
The better circle than
All other circles
Small

And that is when
I see the answer
For Confusion great
And small

That is when I
Know that Truth
Is what tears down
The self-righteous
Fiefdom of the
Blind who lead the blind

For what all seek
Is truly Truth
So far above
Any of the circles
They have known,
The Truth is indeed
A leader strong
Possessing answers

To the quandary of
The day and very hour
In which we live

All we really want to
Find is that Person
We all can trust who,
Unlike fiefdoms with
An idiot at the top,
Proclaims the truth
That really is the truth
And not the normal
Idiot ramblings
Of a fiefdom with an
Idiot at the top of
Self made circles small

Not like the
Fiefdom of the one who's
Goal it was to
Perch atop
To get
A dozen pats upon their back

And when we find
This One who's able
To proclaim the truth
That is the truth,
I hope and pray
We all break the cycle grim
And never let an idiot
At the top again,
But rather let the One
Who we have found
To proclaim the truth

That is the truth,
Because He is the Truth
Be the one we choose
To sit within
Our circle at the top.

---

*And you will know the truth,
and the truth will set you free.
John 8:32*

It Comes With The Job

He who digs a pit will fall into it,
and a serpent will bite him who breaks through a wall.
He who quarries stones is hurt by them,
and he who splits logs is endangered by them.
Ecclesiastes 10:8-9

Should have, could have,
Maybe if only I would have,
Done this or that,
Or maybe even the other!

I thought I had it made
When a good career
I chose,
But then life came
Along and
Delusion faced realities'
Tough stare.

I second guessed decisions,
When life brought me
A challenge
On a plate
Served when I was
Sure things should
Have a better end.

What if I whined:
Oh me oh my,
I am a carpenter and
My hammer
Hit my thumb!

Or maybe
I'm brick layer,
and a brick
Fell on my toe.

Did a big strong
Forestry worker
Trip on a felled tree?
Or did a Vet
Get bitten
By a dog?

And what of that
And maybe more?

All of this
Life stuff,
Large or small,
Is part of
The packaged
Stuff of life
To deal with!

No Whining!
No second guessing!
Just up and at the challenge
Vigor and energy
Is what I'm gifted with today!

Let's go!!!!

But one thing I do:
forgetting what lies behind
and straining forward to what lies ahead,
I press on toward the goal.
Philippians 3:13-14

A Spineless Ineffectual Self

The lips of a fool consume him.
The beginning of the words of his mouth is foolishness,
and the end of his talk is evil madness.
Ecclesiastes 10:12-13.

Inside that tall,
Handsome, very very wealthy,
Stately man
Was a surprisingly
Small minded
Spineless shriveled
Will
That could not discern
The right direction
When in any crisis
Great or small

He never took the time
To care about
The things that really matter:
No scaffolding of truth
Did he erect
No mounting
Structure of character
Supported any of the
Building of his life.

In His bustling
Ego strong
He was so sure it was his
Smarts that brought him
To the top

That looking down
With condescension
On his peers
He mocked them
All

Little knowing
It was his
Imparted gift of life
Mixed with the
Fluke of chance
That got him to where
He is today

Yet he like
Most other bullies
Bold and brash
With arrogant
Self confidence
Still yet terrorizes
All and any
In the throng
That dare bustle
Down along the road of life
Beside him

He does not see
That destiny itself
Gives him a task to care
And look out for those
That are less
Fortunate than his
Own small minded
Tight and lonely
Circle of
Me myself and I

That represents
His shriveled life

There is something
In his mindset small,
That shorts
The current
To reality.
He does not see
What others see
His arrogance
The fodder of
The clouded thinking
He portrays.

Thus
He is
The first
Casualty Of any crisis
Great or small,
And does always
Crumble more
Quickly than the
Rest,
Falling into
His supposed
Attained statehood of
His non-essential,
Ineffectual self.

And like other
Babbling fools
Will one day be
Known finally by all
As irrelevant

Irrelevant as
He really
Always was
In this life
And the next
He will meet
His disconsolate end

I have seen a wicked, ruthless man,
spreading himself like a green laurel tree.
But he passed away, and behold, he was no more;
though I sought him, he could not be found.
Psalm 37:35-36

The fool says in his heart, "There is no God."
Psalm 14:1

Fishing

Cast your bread upon the waters,
for you will find it after many days
He who observes the wind will not sow,
and he who regards the clouds will not reap.
Ecclesiastes 11:1,4.

Can we go fishing for a few minutes together?

The first thing we do is check the weather. Wind speed is crucial because wave height can make our day on the water dangerous, or even capsize our boat! Based on the wind direction and speed we choose our location on a particular body of water, preferably in the lee of the wind.

Boat preparation is next. What type of fish will we target? What rods and reels will we bring? What bait to use? Is the boat gassed up? What other equipment will be needed? Is everything packed and ready to go in the boat?

What about the vehicle to tow the boat to water? Is it gassed up and ready?

The boat and vehicle are ready to go; therefore, we pack a lunch and meet early, very early, the sun has not risen and there is very little traffic on the road. We make our way to the launch point at our destination and back down the ramp. After launching the boat, parking the truck and trailer, we are finally out on the water.

It takes a while to boat out to the proper depth of water and get all the lines out in the water. We are using two downriggers, one dipsy diver and one lead core flat line (the first timers in the boat have no idea what we are doing). Finally, the lines are down.

We are in control of everything we have done to this point, but the rest is not in our control. It is out of our hands. Will the fish bite? Maybe they will, maybe they will not; we cannot control that; some days we catch lots, some days: not! Whatever the outcome we have had a good day. We enjoyed the experience. Why? Because we come home tired but mentally rested and invigorated.

Today you and I are going fishing on the lake called Life. There are some things we can prepare for. So let's do that to the best of our ability. Some things we cannot prepare for. At the end of this day, no matter what the outcome, we can be tired but invigorated at the same time when we know we have done our best.

We don't stay home. We get moving! We do what we can. . . time and chance do the rest!

Whatever the outcome we will have a great day!

Whatever you do, work heartily, as for the Lord.
Colossians 3:23

Whatever your hand finds to do, do it with your might.
Ecclesiastes 9:10

Hiding in Plain Sight

As you do not know the way the spirit comes to the bones in the womb of a woman with child, so you do not know the work of God who makes everything.
Ecclesiastes 11:5

Hiding in plain sight
Was the tactic
Truth deployed
Because this hiding
In plain sight
Reveals one of the
Facts of life:

People who
Want to know
Will know!
People who don't
Care to know
Won't know

That's why
Truth is hidden in
Simple stories
We all understand

Because Truth itself
Will then know
People who
Want to know
Will know!
People who don't

Care to know
Won't know
One look at
A star filled sky
On a very clear night
Tells the truth:
"People who care to
Know it
They will know it!"

But there are
Those who won't know
What they could know
Because people
Who refuse to
Care to know
Won't know

The night sky proclaims
In plain Speech
Not given
To the ear
Explained so plainly
A babe can and does understand

People who
Want to know
Will know!
But people who
Refuse to know
Won't care
To Know
And those who
Refuse to
Care to know
Won't know

There was one with
A pain so deep
And covered with
Dark secrets of the soul
Buried long years
Ago but never opened
. .. and then came Truth
Enjoined to tender care,
Which unlocked the doors
Of darkness
And set the
Prisoner free.

That soul encased
In darkness
Destined for despair

Needed much help
To be set free!
And so help came
Simply hidden
In plain sight!
It gave slow and quiet
Strength
Gained every
One day at a time

Truth sometimes hidden in
Simple stories
We all understand
Hiding in plain sight
Was the tactic
Truth deployed
And promised;
"People who care to
Know Truth,
They will know it!"

*The heavens declare the glory of God,
and the sky above proclaims his handiwork.
There is no speech, nor are there words,
whose voice is not heard.
Their voice goes out through all the earth,
and their words to the end of the world.
Ps 19:1,3-4*

*This is why I speak to them in parables,
because seeing they do not see,
and hearing they do not hear,
nor do they understand. ⋯
But blessed are your eyes, for they see,
and your ears, for they hear.
Mathew 13:11,16*

A Thousand Distant Shores

I walked along the pathways
Of a thousand distant shores
And found my place
On each of them
To look and see
What I could see

I sat and gazed behind
To see the twisted roads
From which I came
And saw the many pathways
That I knew had led me here

Some twists they happened
As a course of living
In this world

And others few were from the
Hateful acts of others
Come my way

Some of the paths
Were dark
Because my selfish stubborn,
Ways prescribed
For me
A broken aching heart

Most of the thousand
Pathways I had walked
I made them on
My own, I did.

I made them
On my own!

I felt the hurt,
Many of those roads had caused.
I knew they bruised me deep inside
And sometimes wondered why they
Happened as they did.

I walked along the pathways
Of a thousand distant shores
And found my place
On each of them
But now instead of looking back
I turned and gazed ahead
To look beyond and see
What I could see
On roads ahead!

And then I saw a broken
Pierc-ed Heart upon a cross
And knew there was another,
Who had faced more pain than I.

Yet in my beyond vision
Understanding that the
Twists and turns He took
Were not because of
Any stubborn, selfish
Act He did,
But rather all the past
And present and yet future
Acts of selfish and
Relentless stupid stubborn
Acts of people just like me.

His hurt was greater
Than mine was
Because it was for me
And all the other sinful selves
That ever walked a twisted road.

And from His wounded hands, His side
There flowed a giving stream of strength
To lovingly impart
Forgiveness for the
Whosoever dropped their guard,
And called upon His name!

And then that day
He took my hand,
I grimaced at the thought:
His hand was pierced!
Just like his heart,
His hand was pierced for me!

And when I put my hand in His
The twists along the road of life
Did not all go away,
But clearly by my side there was
Another who would
Help me in my plight.

I walked along the pathways
Of a thousand distant shores
And found my place
On each of them
And at my side
He walked with me

And even though the paths,
They twisted and they turned,
Somehow all paths
Were paths of peace

My Champion My Warrior My Strong

It is finished!
Was his resurrected start:
He went beyond the grave,
Down the long road
Into the mystic darkness

Past the righteous prisoners
Waiting for "The Day"

He then high stepped
Across a gulf
No departed ever could
And then descending,
Deep, Deep, Down,
Into the chambers of the damned!
To the labyrinth leading
Ever downward
Holding wicked small and great
Within the dungeoned
Gristled dank
Every step He took,
Deliberate to the lowest low!

Erratic, shriveled, gleeful
Dancing demons,
Dared not impede
His progress, nor to touch
The one who now deliberate
Strode the rocky road,
Down, down, down,
To lowest low

His head held high,
Each step closer to the
Huge accusatory chamber
Where paced the creature,
Once a stunning angel,
Now a Snake
And when they looked
Each other in the eye
The one who hissed his way to prominence
Whimpered at the sight of
The nails and wounded side

Slowly my champion
Stretched a nail pierce hand
And took
The keys of death and hell

That snake now slithered
To avoid His strong
And mighty power

No argument was made with
This the long hidden
Wisdom of the Universe
Who won the fight
By yielding to the Father's will
And died upon that cross
Where yipping demons
Danced with glee

"I am"; He said
And when he did
The shriveled serpents' head
Was dealt a mortal blow.
(He still yet writhes in

Final desperate throes of death)
While his demon hordes scampered
To dark corners far beneath
They fled the voice
Of the mighty strong who
All power over darkness
He did possess
In this realm of all the damned

With keys in hand
Ascending quickly past
The eternal prisons of the wicked
He used the speed of light
To up the passage
Cross the gulf,
Where he did meet a cheering throng
Of old Saints who waited
Centuries for that moment
Tucked away as righteous dead
Who knew this day would come
When their strong and mighty
Champion would unlock
Those black gates of hell
Did not prevail
Releasing them to
Rise beside Him at His side

They all darted light speed
Towards the Father up above

Stop!

That whole entourage
Now waiting for a moment
Watching as their

Champion met
Tender Mary
At the tomb.
"Do not touch
Me yet, I will be back. I'm on
My way to show my Hands
My Side to Father up above.
Go tell my brethren and tell
Peter I'm alive and
Back from death"

Then back to the
Task at hand he led
The captives he took captive
To the presence of the
Father where there
As Victor Son
He knelt presenting
Blood for those atoned

They waited long their
Captivity to be
Led captive to
The presence of
The Champion
That called them
As His own

And these who
Now have received
All their reward
They do yet
Cheer me on
They are my witnesses
Who want me

Join them
On my day
When purposed gifts
Given for my tasks
Are all completed
One by one
Life down here on earth.

And may I live today
As though it is my last
And every day thereafter
Knowing my Champion
My Warrior, my Strong
He died upon
That cross and won
The keys of hell and hades
And gave me gifts
That I might be
And do his will
Until I am no more
That day I join the heavenly mighty throng
And you?
If so
You know him
Then yes,
Our Champion did
He gave us gifts
Our Warrior Strong
He did for me and you!

———————

Jesus said to her, "Mary." She turned and said to him in Aramaic, "Rabboni!" (Which means Teacher). Jesus said to her, "Do not cling to me, for I have not yet ascended to the Father; but go to my brothers and say to them, 'I am ascending to my Father and your Father, to my God and your God.'
John 20 16-17

*"When he ascended on high
he led a host of captives,
and he gave gifts to men."
Ephesians 4:8*

When the Way Was Dark and Lonely

*Wisdom gives strength to the wise man
more than ten rulers who are in a city.
Ecclesiastes 7:19*

He walked through
The darkness with me!

Standing on the edge
Of time,
His presence reassured me
All was well,
For . . .
He walked through
The darkness with me!

Teetering precariously,
Perched between time
And the dark unknown;
I looked aghast,
Alone, and wondering?

And then a clear
And glowing comfort
As the scales
On my
Crusty time closed eyes
Saw through the mist.
That. . .
He walked through
The darkness with me!
Standing silent in the

Shadows
Amidst the din of
Urgent babbling voices
Trying to shout me
To a safer path
He stood there strong
And ever glorious
Knowing. . . .
He walked through
The darkness with me!

And then without
A spoken word
Or any explanation
I stepped gingerly
This dangerous pathway
Knowing every step was guided
Knowing surely
Confidently quiet
That His
Strength did lead me
Back into the light
Surely . . .
He walked through
The darkness with me!

What then shall we say to these things? If God is for us, who can be against us? He who did not spare his own Son but gave him up for us all, how will he not also with him graciously give us all things?
Romans 8:31-32

Your Will Be Done!

Many say... My Own Will be Done!
But who will say... Your Will be Done?

Fear God and keep his commandments, for this is the whole duty of man. For God will bring every deed into judgment, with every secret thing, whether good or evil."
Ecclesiastes 12:13-14

So awesome was the sight I trembled
Knees that shook
Bent
My face bowed
Low down to the dusty road
Beneath my feet.

All others trembled
Bowing down
So low down low to the ground~
Until there was no one
As far as eye could see
That stood erect
Or raised their head
To look upon the
Sight displayed before us
in His person

A face that shonne
Brighter than the noonday sun
A robe much brighter
Than the cleanest white.
While eyes that burned with

A champion's stare
Pierced through
The chasmed
Labyrinth channels
Of every prostrate soul

I trembled barely taking
In the thunderous roar
His voice impaling
All His enemies
Choosing of their own accord
To now bow low

I stole a glance!
His feet emanating
Furnaced glowing bronze

Authoritatively planted
On the continent divide
Where're He would

While that strong voice
Yet thundered dark:
"Depart from me, I never knew
You!"

And then most turned and
Of their own accord
Scrambled away
From the awesome
Sight before us
Rushing, plunging over
The spaceless cliff of time
Into the abyss of separation
They themselves desired

Falling downward
Of their own accord
They themselves desired
To flee from Him
Into thick black darkness
Felt for all eternity

To those who fled away
The lamb they slew
Became the one they feared:
Forever lion fierce!
Destructive! Strong!

They bent their knee,
In fear they cowered
Trembling!

And oh, the Pain, for
Those that heard; "Depart from me!"
They fled from Him,
Eternally Alone!
They wished it so!
Ironically,
They wished it so!

Yet to me
and others few and far between,
A gentle hand that touched
Each shoulder
And a voice that whispered
To our quivering hearts:
"Fear not, my children,
No! Fear not!
Arise and come
Into the kingdom
I've prepared."

And then a pathway
Unimaginable and winding
Through flowered meadows
Flowing streams and
Friends that I had known,
For decades we walked together
Towards the city home
Where He promised us
Eternity unfolding
Where we would
Enjoy His presence evermore,
And the creative tasks
He had for us to do
Sustained and knowing
All His love and comfort sweet,

His radiance providing
Rejuvenating light.

For all those
He said belonged to Him.
He evermore shall be
A champion strong
Who touched our
Trembling souls and
Transported in an instant
From dark fear to peace
For all eternity

A place prepared,
For those that know His
Eternal presence
Peace and Joy
and Love

Love
That knows no bounds
Forevermore!

"When I saw him, I fell at his feet as though dead. But he laid his right hand on me, saying, "Fear not, I am the first and the last, and the living one. I died, and behold I am alive forevermore, and I have the keys of Death and Hades."
Revelation 1:17-18

I go and prepare a place for you, I will come again and will take you to myself, that where I am you may be also.
John 14:4

"Enter through the narrow gate. For wide is the gate and broad and easy to travel is the path that leads the way to destruction and eternal loss, and there are many who enter through it.
Matthew 7:13 AMP

May We Find Him

In a quiet
Unexpected moment
God met
Me there

I saw Him
In His promise

I saw Him
In His comfort

He surprised
Me with
His presence.

I saw Him
There.

He is with
Me
Here

And so
May He also
Be with you

Yes,
Be with you

Conclusions

When Jewish King Solomon, came to the throne, he was humbly dependent upon the God of Israel. Although Solomon began a wise, successful, respected, powerful, benevolent spiritual leader, he eventually changed his core values incorporating the corrupt philosophical pagan religious world views of his 700 foreign wives and 300 concubines. The result? He slowly drifted into spiritual blindness, depression, and despair. (*For when Solomon was old his wives turned away his heart after other gods, and his heart was not wholly true to the Lord his God, as was the heart of David his father. 1 Kings 11:4 ESV*). His heart was torn but his wisdom stayed with him.

In contrast the Apostle Paul, arguably the wisest and most respected leader of the early church, stayed true to his core values, increasing in wisdom, influence, and spiritual leadership from the time he met Christ until the time of his death.

At one point in their lives, both Solomon and Paul had very similar outlooks on life. Contrast came as Solomon drifted. Solomon's writings in the book of Ecclesiastes documents his cynical view of God, and despairing view of life; a man who once knew God but was now living far from God. In contrast, from the moment Paul met the resurrected Christ he wrote much of his ever-growing personal relationship with God and positive triumphant view of life.

Hopefully these pages have allowed us to feel "Wisdom in Contrast"!

Solomon concluded his writing:
> *"Meaningless! Meaningless!" says the Teacher.*
> *"Everything is meaningless!"*
> *Ecclesiastes 12:8 NIV*

Alternatively, Paul declares:
> *"In conclusion, be strong in the Lord*
> *[draw your strength from Him and be empowered*
> *through your union with Him]*
> *and in the power of His [boundless] might."*
> *Ephesians 6:10 AMP*

On a personal note, there are times in my life when I chose Solomon's world of self-indulgence, and like Solomon suffered greatly for it; however, it has also been my experience to choose like Paul, knowing the true life-giving-wisdom and the resulting triumphant joy produced by it!

May the contrasts by comparison stay with you: *choose wisely my friend, choose wisely!*

About the author:

Victor Grieco spent two decades as an ordained minister prior to entering the financial services field where he attained designations as a Certified Financial Planning professional (CFP), an Elder Planning Counsellor (EPC) and most recently as a Master Financial Advisor–Philanthropy (MFA-P).

In this artistic offering, he shares lessons learned from church life, business, family life, and the writings of ancients renowned for their wisdom.

It is Victor's hope that the reader experiences the elusive contrasting *emotions of wisdom*. His goal? Inspiration towards wise choices in every life endeavor!

Victor lives in Kitchener Ontario Canada. You can contact him here: **vguy1000@gmail.com**

Manufactured by Amazon.ca
Bolton, ON